LIV TYLER

A Real-Life Reader Biography

Sue Boulais

Mitchell Lane Publishers, Inc.
P.O. Box 619
Bear, Delaware 19701

Real-Life Reader Biographies

Selena	Robert Rodriguez	Mariah Carey	Rafael Palmeiro
Tommy Nuñez	Trent Dimas	Cristina Saralegui	Andres Galarraga
Oscar De La Hoya	Gloria Estefan	Jimmy Smits	Mary Joe Fernandez
Cesar Chavez	Chuck Norris	Sinbad	Paula Abdul
Vanessa Williams	Celine Dion	Mia Hamm	Sammy Sosa
Brandy	Michelle Kwan	Rosie O'Donnell	Shania Twain
Garth Brooks	Jeff Gordon	Mark McGwire	Salma Hayek
Sheila E.	Hollywood Hogan	Ricky Martin	Britney Spears
Arnold Schwarzenegger	Jennifer Lopez	Kobe Bryant	Derek Jeter
Steve Jobs	Sandra Bullock	Julia Roberts	Robin Williams
Jennifer Love Hewitt	Keri Russell	Sarah Michelle Gellar	**Liv Tyler**
Melissa Joan Hart	Drew Barrymore	Alicia Silverstone	Katie Holmes
Winona Ryder	Alyssa Milano	Freddie Prinze, Jr.	Enrique Iglesias
Christina Aguilera			

Library of Congress Cataloging-in-Publication Data
Boulais, Sue.
     Liv Tyler/Sue Boulais.
         p. cm. — (A real-life reader biography)
     Includes index.
     ISBN 1-58415-041-6
     1. Tyler, Liv. 2. Motion picture actors and actresses—United States—Biography—Juvenile literature. [1. Tyler, Liv. 2. Actors and actresses. 3. Women—Biography.] I. Title. II. Series.
PN2287.T93 B68 2000
791.43'028'092—dc21
    [B]
                                                  00-057729

ABOUT THE AUTHOR: Sue Boulais is a freelance writer/editor based in Orlando, Florida. She has published numerous books, including *Famous Astronauts* (Media Materials) and *Hispanic American Achievers* (Frog Publications). Previously, she served as an editor for *Weekly Reader* and Hartcourt Brace.

PHOTO CREDITS: cover: Corbis; p. 4 Archive Photos; p. 12 Archive Photos; p. 17 Globe Photos; p. 19 Corbis; p. 21 Fox Searchlight; p. 26 Corbis

ACKNOWLEDGMENTS: The following story has been thoroughly researched, and to the best of our knowledge, represents a true story. While every possible effort has been made to ensure accuracy, the publisher will not assume liability for damages caused by inaccuracies in the data, and makes no warranty on the accuracy of the information contained herein. This story has not been authorized by Liv Tyler or any of her representatives.

Table of Contents

Chapter 1
It Was the '70s

Liv Tyler was born in New York City on July 1, 1977, into the wild, noisy, chaotic world of acid rock music. Her mother, Bebe Buell, was a striking young model, caught up in the New York drink-and-drug whirl. Bebe had relationships with several big-name musicians—Elvis Costello, Todd Rundgren, and Steven Tyler. She became pregnant with Liv when she was involved with Steve Tyler following a disagreement with Rundgren.

At the time, Tyler was totally absorbed in a battle with heroin and

> **Liv Tyler was born into the wild, noisy, chaotic world of acid rock music.**

alcohol. Bebe herself was slowly becoming aware that her lifestyle was dangerous and destructive. When she found that she was pregnant, Bebe left Tyler, and returned to Rundgren. Although she was frightened and confused, she was certain of one thing. She did not want to raise her child in the atmosphere that surrounded her. Bebe later described that time before Liv's birth as "…hell. I was very young, and it was very scary…. I didn't want life to be going like this."

Bebe persuaded Rundgren to say he was the baby's father. So, when the baby was born, the name Bebe put on the birth certificate was Liv Rundgren. For several months after Liv's birth, she and her mother stayed in New York City with Rundgren. However, Bebe and Rundgren finally parted. Bebe and Liv moved to Portland, Maine, where Bebe had relatives. Bebe wanted more security for Liv, as well as for herself.

So Liv spent her childhood years far from the '70s New York City rock scene in a much more stable environment. "It was just me and my mother, my aunt, my uncle, and two cousins in a big house," Liv says. "We'd mow the lawn and run with the cows and . . . have barbecues."

Liv spent several years with her grandparents as well. They lived in Fairfax, Virginia, a community with many cultural riches. "[My grandparents would] take me to the theater and museums," Liv recalls. "They were very much more conservative than my mom, who was . . . . a rock and roller."

Although many people feel her upbringing was unconventional, Liv wonders "What's conventional?" She is quick to remind interviewers that she had spent most of her first 12 years in Portland, Maine, surrounded by family and friends.

During Liv's childhood, Bebe stayed in touch with Todd Rundgren, and also contacted Steven Tyler, who was still battling drug addiction. Bebe

She took Liv and moved to Maine to be near relatives.

Bebe raised Liv as Todd Rundgren's daughter.

and Tyler reached an agreement to tell Liv the truth about her relationship to Tyler when she was 18. In the meantime, Bebe raised Liv as Rundgren's daughter, and the little girl regarded him as her father. Liv has explained that she and Todd Rundgren were very close, and that he was a "huge influence" in her life. "He's an intellectual; he taught me about music," she said. In fact, he was one of the men most important to her.

With a "rock and roller" for a mom, Liv got to go to rock concerts as well as theaters and museums. When she was ten years old, Liv went with Bebe to a Rundgren concert in Boston, Massachusetts. There, she first met Steven Tyler, and began to wonder about the likenesses between them.

Chapter 2
Steven and Mia

After Todd's concert, Liv and her mother went backstage to congratulate him and visit with other concert-goers. Liv remembers feeling "gawky" as only a ten-year-old can. (She insists that, as a little girl, she had "huge hands and feet; I was awkward, totally chubby.") Then, she was introduced to Steven Tyler, who was also backstage. She recalls feeling an instant "connection," and how he made her feel important. "He began buying me Shirley Temples [a non-alcoholic drink]. . . He was . . . old-fashioned."

The first time Liv met Steve Tyler she recalls an instant connec—tion.

Liv found it a little puzzling that Tyler paid attention to her. But it didn't worry her. She could see that Tyler knew her mother, and she just thought he was an old friend.

But Tyler remained a part of Liv's life after the concert. He began to send her presents and stuffed animals. Whenever Tyler and his rock group, Aerosmith, played in the area, Bebe would take Liv to the concerts. "We'd see him play," remembers Liv, "and hang out with him."

Liv noticed a likeness to Steve's daughter, Mia.

In the next couple of years, Liv's curiosity grew. She noticed that she and Tyler had facial features that were exactly the same, that they "had the same legs," the same thick, dark hair.

When Liv was 12, she and Bebe went to an Aerosmith concert. Backstage, Liv met Mia, Tyler's daughter. "We were both wearing Aerosmith T-shirts and we both had terrible perms and were really chubby," says Liv. But what really made Liv stop and think was the fact that, even though

Mia was about a year younger, the two girls "were like identical twins."

That meeting with Mia escalated Liv's curiosity and puzzlement. "I just . . . knew," Liv states. When she asked her mother if Steven Tyler was her father, Bebe admitted it. She also explained that Mia's mother was model Cyrinda Foxe, who had been Tyler's wife for several years after Bebe and Tyler had broken up. Like Bebe, Cyrinda had wanted a more normal life for her daughter. Cyrinda had left Tyler and raised Mia in New Hampshire. Mia, like Liv, was "a normal kid."

Liv was delighted. Not only was her curiosity satisfied, but she also realized she'd have more relatives. She remembers, "I was just so excited. I thought, I'm going to have two dads and more brothers and sisters and all these grandparents." Christmas would be great.

Liv loved her "extended family." The relationships might have seemed unconventional to many, but not to Liv.

"I just knew," Liv states.

Liv with her biological father, Steve Tyler

Her view was that "[my upbringing] was loving. I had these different worlds, [Maine, Virginia, New York City] and it made me a kind of multipersonality."

Liv stated very firmly that she was not upset with her father for not being around when she was a child. "He [Tyler] wouldn't have been in my life anyway. He was a drug addict. It wasn't until he decided to take that step to sobriety that he changed his life forever. . . . [now] he's my friend and I enjoy him a lot."

Soon after the discovery of her new family, another big change took place. Liv and her mother moved from Portland, Maine back to New York City.

> **"He [Tyler] wouldn't have been in my life anyway."**

Chapter 3
Life In New York

Liv and her mother moved back to New York City when Liv was 12.

When Liv and her mother came back to New York City, Liv was 12. They settled in an apartment in Greenwich Village, a section in lower Manhattan best known for its colorful population of actors, artists, and musicians. Liv started school at York Prep in New York City's Upper East Side.

During her early teen years, Liv began to lose her awkward chubbiness. She grew tall and slender, her face lost its roundness. By the time she was 14, she finally "fit" her hands and feet, which she had always considered "huge."

Liv didn't really notice the changes, but family friend Paulina Porizkova did. Paulina, a supermodel for cosmetics and perfumes, took some photos of Liv after coaxing the young girl out of baggy clothes. Paulina put the photos together in a portfolio, and, without telling Liv, contacted a number of modeling agencies and magazines.

Paulina's photos appeared as a full-page spread in *Interview* magazine. Within a few months, Liv appeared in lingerie, swimsuit, and clothing ads in *Seventeen* and *Mademoiselle*, popular fashion magazines.

For the next couple of years, Liv was one of the most sought-after teen models in the industry. She flew to glamorous locations around the world for fashion shoots. She starred in clothing and cosmetic commercials. During the early part of her modeling career, Liv felt very lucky. "It was really a great thing," she said of that time. "I was traveling and making money."

Paulina put together photos of Liv and contacted modeling agencies and magazines.

After a while, modeling lost its appeal.

After a while, however, the modeling life began to lose appeal for her. Liv found that she had no time for the regular everyday activities that her school friends enjoyed. "I was traveling, and the other kids thought I had these special privileges," Liv remembers. "But to me, they had the special privileges: They could go to school all day and go home and watch TV and do their thing, while I was all over the place."

Liv became aware that many people wanted to be her friend just because she was a model. She remarked, "Everyone wants to be your friend. But why? Because you're pretty? You have to keep the radar up."

After two years of "keeping the radar up," Liv was more than ready to quit. She was bored with the travel— and she was bored with the way modeling was only concerned with how a person looks. "It [modeling] was just too external [the outside of things, what you can see]." Liv added that she had become bored, and that internals—why

> **"What makes people beautiful is their originality, the character within them—selves."**

people are what they are, and why they do what they do—were far more interesting to her.

"It's weird," she says. ". . . a lot of people don't look like [models] and they shouldn't . . . it shouldn't be . . . [that] the only way to be beautiful is to look like some girl in a picture." She adds, "Everybody is born different. What makes people beautiful is their originality, the character within themselves."

She also didn't like the fact that modeling focused so much on appearance. So, while on a modeling assignment in Venezuela, Liv mentioned to her mother that she'd like to try acting. "I was just curious," she says. She decided that she'd sign up with an acting coach and get some books on acting.

Before Liv could even get to the library, however, she got a call from a movie agent. He'd read about her in a *New York Times* article about children of the famous. The agent wanted her to audition for the movie *Silent Fall*, a psychological thriller starring Richard Dreyfus.

As Liv grew older, she became a striking beauty.

Chapter 4
The Movie Scene

Liv's early film roles were in small movies with well-known directors.

The *New York Times* article marked Liv's "official" discovery by the film world. Mom Bebe announced that she would manage Liv's career. Bebe had no intention of allowing Liv to work in any "slasher" movies; "you know," Bebe explains, "the stalking and the violence and the blood." So Liv's early film roles were in smaller, less-risky movies with well-known directors. Within months, Bebe and Liv had agreed that Liv would work on three movies: *Silent Fall, Upstate Story*, and *Empire Records*.

Silent Fall was released in 1994, and the other two appeared during 1995.

None of the films won much praise from reviewers, but the movies did put Liv squarely on center stage as one of Hollywood's newest stars-in-the-making.

Then, in June, 1996, *Stealing Beauty* and *Heavy* were released. Both films won critical raves. *Stealing Beauty*, directed by world-renowned Bernardo Bertolucci, had been entered in

In 1996, Liv starred in Bernardo Bertolucci's film, Stealing Beauty.

competition at that year's Cannes Film Festival, and Liv was the toast of the town. *Heavy* was also a prize-winner: it had received the Grand Jury award at the 1995 Sundance Film Festival. Reviews of both films focused on Liv's performances, and her potential and presence. Her "innocence and lack of inhibition" made her outstanding in *Stealing Beauty*; "sweetly tentative" in *Heavy*.

Some reviewers felt her beauty and talent were being misused, that her roles—such as that of Lucy in *Stealing Beauty*—made her an object of desire. When asked how she felt about that, she replied, "I [don't] understand how a movie about a young girl, especially me, could be interesting for two hours."

Once again, her photograph graced the pages of magazines and newspapers. Now, though, she wasn't only featured in fashion magazines such as *Seventeen* and *Mirabella*; she also appeared on the covers of *Entertainment Weekly* and *People*, in two and three-page

Liv won rave reviews for her perform- ances in her early films.

articles in *Time* and *Cosmopolitan*. Interviewers praised her confidence and assurance, and the way she seemed to be enjoying her success. They also expressed surprise at her honesty, level-headedness and straightforwardness. Whether a reporter questioned her about her acting or her family life, Liv had an answer.

Liv asserted that she was no longer involved in the teen club scene in New York and Los Angeles. "I'm over that . . . When I was like, fifteen and living in New York, I used to go out . . . But not now. . . . everyone's there to pick one another up . . . and get drunk . . . that's not life, because suddenly you wake up miserable and say, 'What am I going to do?'"

Liv displayed absolutely no hesitation when asked about her views on drugs. "I knew at a very early age that drugs are terrifying, terrible things. I've never been interested in them. They're just not cool." When talking

Liv has never been into drugs. "I knew at a very early age that drugs are terrifying, terrible things. I've never been interested in them. They're just not cool."

about her father's addictions, she labeled heroin the "absolute devil," adding that Tyler had been clean and sober for a decade or more. "He gets more beautiful every day."

Liv knows that getting an education is very important, and wants to make up for lost years of learning. "I'd love to go to college." She says. ". . . I've missed learning about literature and art. I'm a terrible speller. I'm always learning. [My] friends are. . . twenty. I always say 'Go to school. . . just a bit of knowledge helps . . . instead of sitting around and talking and smoking pot and going to clubs."

Within six months of the release of *Stealing Beauty* and *Heavy*, Liv was solidly established as a young actress whose presence on the film screen was strong—and growing. Film critics, directors, and other actors and actresses agreed that Liv gave the appearance of being truly at ease with herself.

She was also solidly established as a young woman who knew what she

Liv knows that education is very important.

didn't want and where she *didn't* want to be. Liv wouldn't get caught in the lifestyle of the '70s, the lifestyle of many in her parents' generation. A *Cosmopolitan* interview described her as a teenager who had managed "to acquire a core of stability, inner strength, and sanity that was missing in most of the people around her." Actor-director Tom Hanks, who worked with Liv in the film *That Thing You Do*, observed, "This is an extremely well-grounded girl. She's the oldest 18-year-old I've ever encountered."

Those who looked for indications that Liv's behavior at 18 would be like her parents' behavior had been at 18 couldn't find any. Liv acknowledged that she was different from her parents—and her parents acknowledged it, too. Liv reported a conversation she had had with Steven Tyler: "I was talking to my dad this morning and he said to me, like, "Where did you come from? You're like an animal from another planet!'" Mom Bebe remarked,

Those who looked for indications that Liv's behavior at 18 would be like her parents' behavior at 18 couldn't find any.

"Let's put it this way. Liv admires [actress] Jodie Foster. I admired Anita Pallenberg [a '70s girl whose fame rested on hanging out, groupie-style, with Keith Richards and the Rolling Stones]."

Liv rounded out 1996 by completing work in three more films. She appeared in a cameo role in *Everybody Says I Love You*, a Woody

Liv starred with Johnathan Schaech in That Thing You Do.

Allen film. Actor Tom Hanks cast her as the girlfriend of a '60s rock-and-roll musician in *That Thing You Do*, and she played the youngest of three sisters in *Inventing the Abbotts.* Her scenes in Allen's movie were cut because the film's first cut ran more than three hours. But Liv's parts in the other two movies were hefty, and added to her acting reputation.

At the end of the year, Liv was tired and wanted some time off. After all, she had worked straight for a little more than a year. What she wanted, she said was some down time with herself in New York City. "I can't wait for someone to honk at me and . . . be just one out of a million."

By the end of 1996, Liv needed to take some time off.

Chapter 5
Off and On

At 18, Liv moved into an apartment of her own.

During her time off, Liv moved out of the Greenwich Village apartment into a place of her own. Like many 18-year-olds, she decorated it herself, bringing, she says, "my stuff [that] was scattered in storage or in other places." The finished product thrilled her: ". . . it's so beautiful. I have a fireplace, and I've been cooking dinner and lunches for all my friends. It's so nice to settle down!"

Even though Liv spent much of 1997 getting her life organized, she kept a lookout for interesting film roles. At one point, she reported reading a script a day! She signed to work on several during 1998: *Armageddon, Cookie's Fortune* and *Onegin* (own-YAY-gin).

Being back at work meant that Liv was also back in the limelight, a whole year older and, seemingly, even more years mature. She made no bones about the fact that she liked aging. "It [becoming older] feels fantastic . . . insecurities that teenage years bring on start to go away a little bit. I've always had these fantasies of being a grandmother with really long white hair. I think it's important to embrace [growing old]. . . "

Her work in the three films was well received, for the most part. Reviewers and critics pointed out that Liv's acting was becoming increasingly rich with nuances, and that it still seemed effortless. Most voiced the hope that better roles would be available to her as she matured.

By 1999, Liv was ready for another break—not just from film-making this time, but from the constant glare of the spotlight. She admitted freely that she

She has enjoyed getting older.

"loathed the Hollywood hoopla" that other actors and actresses live for. "I'm only 21, and I want a chance to be a kid," she explained. Then she added a statement that echoed one made during her modeling years: "I've gained so many things from working, but I did miss out on those years of not being conscious of what anyone thinks of you and just being a kid."

As the new millennium began, Liv was lying low—and enjoying the quiet life. "It's nice to be able to go home and decorate your apartment and hang out with your family and go to the museum and discover interests," she maintains. "When you're working, it's difficult to finish a book, and you feel like such an ignoramus all the time."

Perhaps one interest that Liv inherited from her product-of-the-'70s parents is her love of music. Her most prized possession is a 1954 jukebox; on it she plays everything from country western—Patsy Cline and Hank Williams—to R&B's classic ladies—Billie

Holliday and Etta James. And of course, she loves rock and roll. How could she not? It's in her blood.

During an interview with *Cosmopolitan* magazine in 1996, Liv said, "I just hope my decisions about my career, about my life, are better than a lot of people's I know." So far, she's doing just fine. And most predict she'll be able to "keep it up," and build a career—and a life—to be proud of.

Filmography

Onegin (1999)
Cookie's Fortune (1999)
Armageddon (1998)
Inventing the Abbotts (1997)
That Thing You Do! (1996)
Stealing Beauty (1996)
Empire Records (1995)
Heavy (1995)
Upstate Story (1995)
Silent Fall (1994)

Chronology

- Born July 1, 1977, in New York City; mother: Bebe Buell; father: Steve Tyler
- Grew up in Maine and Virginia; raised as Todd Rundgren's daughter
- At the age of 12, discovers that Steve Tyler is her biological father
- 1989, moves back to New York City with her mother
- 1991, begins modeling
- 1994, appears in her first movie, *Silent Fall*
- 1995, moves out on her own
- 1996, stars in her "breakthrough" movie, *Stealing Beauty*
- 1999, stars in *Onegin* and *Cookie's Fortune*

Index